Note to Parents and Teachers

The SCIENCE STARTERS series introduces key science vocabulary and concepts to young children while encouraging them to discover and understand the world around them. The series works as a set of graded readers in three levels.

LEVEL 3: READ ALONE These books can be read alone or as part of guided or group reading. Each book has three sections:

• Information pages that introduce key concepts. Key words appear in bold for easy recognition on pages where the related science concepts are explained.
• A lively story that recalls this vocabulary and encourages children to use these words when they talk and write.
• A quiz asks children to look back and recall what they have read.

GEMS, METALS, and MINERALS looks at ROCKS and SOIL. Below are some answers and activities related to the questions on the information spreads that parents, carers, and teachers can use to discuss and develop further ideas and concepts:

p. 4 *What materials have been used to build your home?* Ask children to make a list sorting materials into natural and manmade materials, e.g. bricks, concrete, wood, slate.

p. 6 *Right now, what are the different layers below you?* Encourage children to think layer by layer, e.g. grass, soil, rock, hot rock below the crust, hot metal at Earth's core.

p. 11 *What else is dug out from mines?* e.g. fuels such as coal; ores containing metals such as iron, copper, and gold; rocks containing gems such as diamonds and emeralds.

p. 15 *What other things can you think of that are made of metal?* Ask children to think about why metals are suited to certain uses, e.g. gold and silver for jewelry; iron and steel for buildings, cars, and tools; tin and aluminum for cans; copper for electric wires.

p. 17 *Where do you think are good places to look for erosion?* Places where wind and water can easily wear away rocks, e.g. on a beach, riverbanks, exposed places such as cliffs, and mountains. Point out that you can also see erosion on buildings, e.g. pollution, wind, and water wear away bricks and stone on houses, statues etc.

p. 19 *Can you see the different things that make up the soil?* Ask children to make a vocabulary list of different elements in the soil, e.g. minerals: clay, mud, sand, and pebbles, and organic particles: sticks, leaves, roots, bone, hair etc.

p. 21 *What plants can you think of that live in a dry desert?* e.g. a cactus stores water in stems, mesquite has long roots 80 feet (25 m) long, Desert lily springs to life when rain falls.

ADVISORY TEAM

Educational Consultant
Andrea Bright—Science Coordinator, Trafalgar Junior School

Literacy Consultant
Jackie Holderness—former Senior Lecturer in Primary Education, Westminster Institute, Oxford Brookes University

Series Consultants
Anne Fussell—Early Years Teacher and University Tutor, Westminster Institute, Oxford Brookes University

David Fussell—C.Chem., FRSC

CONTENTS

© Aladdin Books Ltd 2008

Designed and produced by
Aladdin Books Ltd

First published in
the United States in 2008 by
Stargazer Books
c/o The Creative Company
123 South Broad Street
P.O. Box 227, Mankato,
Minnesota 56002

Printed in the United States
All rights reserved

Editor/ Designer: Jim Pipe
Series Design: Flick, Book
Design & Graphics

Thanks to:
The pupils of Trafalgar
Infants School for appearing as
models in this book.

**Library of Congress
Cataloging-in-Publication Data**

Hewitt, Sally, 1949-
    Rocks and soil /
    by Sally Hewitt.
        p. cm. -- (Science starters)
    Includes index.
    ISBN 978-1-59604-138-7
    (alk. paper)
    1. Rocks--Juvenile literature.
    2. Soils--Juvenile literature.
    I. Title.

QE432.2.H49 2007
552--dc22

    2007009207

Photocredits:
l-left, r-right, b-bottom, t-top,
c-center, m-middle
Cover tl & tr, 2bl, 5bc & br, 8b, 9ml,
10br, 12m, 14 all, 15ml, 16br, 18b,
19m, 20tr, 21br, 22, 23tl & ml, 29tr,
31ml, mr & br—istockphoto.com.
Cover tr, 2ml, 4t, 5tl, 10bl, 11tr,
15br, 17mr, 31tr & bcr—Corbis.
Cover b, 18tr, 23br, 24 all, 25tr &
br, 26-27 all, 28tl & mr, 29ml & br,
30tl—Jim Pipe. 2tl, 9tr & br, 30br—
Marc Arundale/Select Pictures. 3,
11m—Caterpillar. 4mr— Flick Smith.
4br, 5tc, 25ml, 28bl— Ingram
Publishing. 5tr, 16t, 17t— Photodisc.
5bl, 19tr—DAJ. 6br—TongRo. 7tr,
10m, 21t—Stockbyte. 7b—John
Deere. 8tr, 17br, 31bcl—Corel.13m—
Brand X. 15tr—EU. 19bl—Select
Pictures. 20b—USDA.

SCIENCE STARTERS

LEVEL
3

ROCKS AND SOIL

Gems, Metals, and Minerals

by Sally Hewitt

Stargazer Books

ROCKS

Uluru

Materials are what things are made of.
Some materials are natural.
Some are made by humans.

Rocks are natural materials
that cover our planet, Earth.
Pebbles and stones are
small pieces of **rock**.

Pebbles

Uluru (Ayers Rock) is a huge
piece of sandstone **rock** in Australia.

Bricks look like rock but are
made by humans. What
materials have been used to
build your home? Are they
natural or manmade?

4

Concrete block

Rocks can be hard or soft, rough or smooth.
Rocks come in all kinds of colors.
We use them in different ways.

Building
Marble is a strong building material.

Pottery
Clay is made into pots.

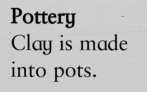

Chalk
Soft, white chalk is used for writing.

Minerals
Pencil leads are made from soft graphite.

Ores
Metals such as gold and iron are found in rocks.

Fuel
We burn coal for fuel.

THE EARTH'S CRUST

Planet **Earth** is a huge ball of rock and metal. The center of the ball is hot metal.

Around the center are layers of hot, liquid rock. On the surface is a hard layer of rock called the **crust**.

The ground under your feet is the rocky **crust**. But the rocks may be covered over with soil or grass.

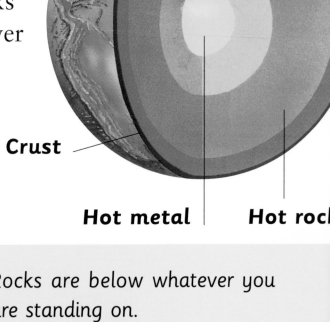

Crust

Hot metal   **Hot rock**

Rocks are below whatever you are standing on.

Right now, what are the different layers below you? What are these boys standing on?

Earth's rocky **crust** is 19 miles (30 km) deep. So most rock is hidden underground.

Diggers dig out rock and soil to make a deep pit to support a tall building.

Digger

Rocks can also be covered by water. Some of the tallest mountains and deepest valleys on Earth lie under the ocean.

SORTING ROCKS

Rocks such as chalk and sandstone are **soft**. They crumble and wear away in the rain and wind.

In places like Monument Valley in Arizona, **hard** rock remains standing. The **soft** rock around it has worn away.

Chalk cliffs battered by the sea crumble and wear away.

Monument Valley

Collect some rocks and find out about them. **Sort rocks** by color. Chalk is white. Slate is gray.

Which rocks are shiny?

Pumice

Most rocks sink in water. Pumice is full of air bubbles.

Put pumice in water and watch it float. It is the only rock that floats.

Find out if your rocks are hard or soft. Rub two rocks together. Which rocks crumble?

Drop water onto the rocks. Does it soak in or roll off?

TOUGH ROCKS

Strong, **tough** rocks are used for building.
They do not wear away like soft rock.
Granite is a **tough** rock. It becomes
smooth and shiny when it is polished.

Granite castle

Slate roof

Flat sheets of
waterproof
slate are used
for making
roof tiles.

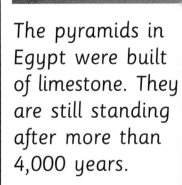

The pyramids in
Egypt were built
of limestone. They
are still standing
after more than
4,000 years.

Tough rocks such as marble are dug out of the ground in quarries.

Marble has been used as a building material for about 2,000 years.

Marble can be carved. This statue was carved from marble 500 years ago.

Marble statue

Quarry

Rocks are also dug out from mines deep underground. Gold is a metal found in rocks underground. What else is dug out from mines?

MINERALS

Rocks are made up of different **minerals**.
We use these **minerals** in all kinds of ways.

Ancient cave painters made their paints from
colored **minerals**. They used charcoal for
black paint, iron oxide for red, chalk
for white, and ocher for yellow. **Cave painting**

Scrape chalk into a powder.
Mix the chalk powder with a little
egg yolk to make white paint.
Now do the same with charcoal to
make black paint. Paint a picture.

Many things in your home have been made from **minerals** found in rocks.

Glass is made from the **mineral** quartz which is found in sand. Quartz is also used in watches to control their speed.

Silicone chips in computers are made from a **mineral** called silica.

Computer

Talc

Talcum powder and some crayons are made from a very soft **mineral** called talc.

13

GEMS, CRYSTALS, AND METALS

You can find treasure buried inside rocks.

Rocks are made of minerals. Sometimes minerals form transparent **crystals** that sparkle in the light.

Gems such as diamonds, rubies, and emeralds are **crystals**.

Crystal

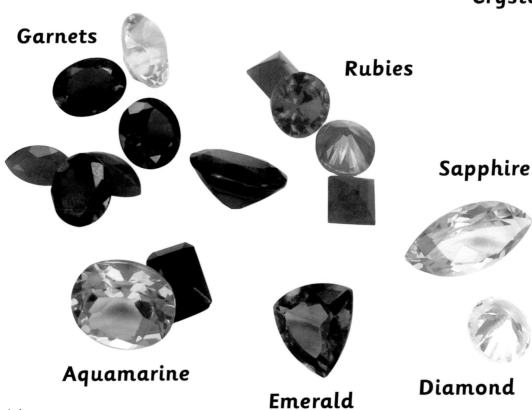

Garnets

Rubies

Sapphire

Aquamarine

Emerald

Diamond

14

Minerals can form **metal ores** in rocks.

The **metal ore** is heated in a furnace to get the **metal** out. Iron **ore** is used to make iron and steel.

Gold and silver are precious **metals** used to make jewelry.

Gold nuggets   **Furnace**

Iron and steel are strong metals used to make bridges.

What other things can you think of that are made of metal?

EROSION AND LAVA

Wind wears away rocks

Rocks don't stay the same forever. They are always being broken down, changed, and made into new rocks.

Ice, wind, and rain wear away rocks and break them into tiny pieces. This is called **erosion**.

Rivers carry the pieces out to sea where they build up very slowly to make new rock.

A glacier is a river of ice. It carves out a valley in the rock.

Volcano

Lava

When liquid rock called
lava bursts through a hole in
the earth's crust, it forms
a **volcano**.

Lava cools, turns into rock,
and builds a new mountain.

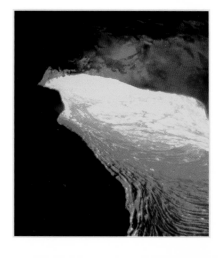

Wind and water erosion can
create amazing rock shapes.
Where do you think are good
places to look for erosion?

17

SOIL

Soil is made up of tiny pieces of rock, stones, and the remains of dead plants and animals.

Worms, beetles, and other animals break up the **soil** and help to make it full of air.

Dead plants in the **soil** make it rich for growing plants.

Digging soil

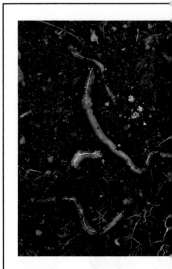

Worms, ants, and earwigs are animal that live in soil.

Soil is different depending on the kind of rock it was made from.

You can find out what is in the **soil** near where you live. Always wash your hands after touching **soil**.

Spread out some dry soil on white paper. Look at it through a magnifying glass.

Can you see the different things that make up the soil?

SOIL FOR LIFE

Soil is like a skin that covers the earth's rocky crust. On a farm, it covers the fields.

Soil is very important to life on Earth. Most plants grow in soil. Their roots suck up water and minerals from the soil.

Roots in soi

Wheat field

Loamy soil

Clay soil is heavy and dark.
It doesn't let water run through it easily.
It gets soggy and full of puddles.

Sandy soil is light and crumbly.
Water can flow through it easily.
It dries out very quickly.

Loamy soil is a mixture of clay, sand, silt, and dead plants. It is very good for growing plants.

Some plants can grow in poor soil. Mountain plants live in cracks in the rocks.

What plants can you think of that live in a dry desert?

21

FOSSILS AND FUELS

Rocks called **fossils** were once the bones and shells of animals that died millions of years ago.

Layers of mud covered the dead animal and pressed down on it heavily.
Over millions of years, the animal turned to rock and became a **fossil**.

Fossils of sea creatures called ammonites are often found in rocks.

Ammonite

Ammonite fossil

Coal

Oil rig

Plants and animals that died millions of years ago also turned into **fuels** such as coal, oil, and gas. We burn these **fuels** for energy.

Coal is mined from underground rocks. Oil and gas are found in rocks underground and under the sea.

Oil wells are drilled in the seabed or ground. Giant tankers deliver oil all over the world.

You can find fossils hidden in rocks on beaches and quarries.

Go fossil hunting safely. Always go with an adult. Beware of crumbling rocks and wear strong boots.

23

TREASURE HUNT

Look out for ideas about rocks and soil.

Hugh and Luke were looking at Uncle Jim's rock collection. "Where did you find all these rocks?" asked Luke.

"I found that rock in the backyard," said Uncle Jim. "It's a piece of flint. Be careful. It has sharp edges."

"Stone Age people used to make arrows and axes from flint, didn't they?" asked Hugh. "That's right," said Uncle Jim.

"This rock is shiny," said Hugh. "It looks like gold!" said Luke.

"It's called 'fool's gold' because it isn't gold at all," said Uncle Jim.

24

"That rock looks like a seashell," said Luke.

"Ooh, a fossil," said Hugh. "Let me see!"
"I found it near here," said Uncle Jim.

"Where?" asked Luke and Hugh.

"I'll show you. Let's go on a treasure hunt!" said Uncle Jim.
They put on strong shoes.
Uncle Jim packed a magnifying glass.

"Walk slowly and look carefully. You are walking on rocks everywhere you go," said Uncle Jim.

"I'm walking on pavement," said Luke.
"But what's underneath?" asked Uncle Jim.

"Rocks!" said Hugh.

Uncle Jim lived near the coast

"Why are we going to the beach? I thought we were looking for rocks!" said Hugh.

Uncle Jim picked up a handful of pebbles. "Pebble are rocks worn smooth and round by the sea," he said.

"Is sand rock too?" asked Luke.

"Yes. Sand is tiny bits of rocks and shells. The weather and the sea ground them into tiny pieces," said Uncle Jim.

"So these pebbles will turn into sand one day," said Hugh. "Look at all the different colors."

26

Luke found a rock pool. "Why haven't these rocks turned into pebbles or sand?" he asked.

"Because they are harder and take longer to wear away," said Uncle Jim.

"Where will we find treasure?" said Luke. "Up there in the cliffs," said Uncle Jim.

"I've found some treasure already," said Hugh. He showed Uncle Jim some pieces of rock with crystal in them.

"I'm going to find better treasure than that!" said Luke.

"Those cliffs look stripy!" said Luke.

"You can see different layers of rock where the sea has worn away the cliffs," said Uncle Jim.

Luke and Hugh ran toward the cliffs.

"Stay with me," called Uncle Jim. "Don't go near the bottom of the cliffs in case of a rock fall."

The children found some rocks and Uncle Jim opened them with his rock hammer.

But they didn't find anything inside.

"Maybe there's gold in this rock," said Luke.

"I think it might be hiding a
different kind of treasure,"
said Uncle Jim smiling.
He split the rock open.

"Ooh!" said Hugh. "A fossil!
Just like the one you showed us."

"It's an ammonite, about 250 million years old,"
said Uncle Jim. "It's the best treasure I've ever
found!" said Luke.

"There's something else you
should see," said Uncle Jim.

"We need to climb this slope.
Watch out for crumbly soil!"

"It's a dinosaur footprint,"
shouted Hugh. "It must be
millions of years old, too."

Then they climbed carefully
back down to the beach.

Back down on the beach,
the tide was coming in.
"We'll be trapped!" joked Luke.

As they walked back, the boys
kept on looking at the ground.

"I'm going to look for interesting
rocks wherever I go," said Luke.

"Back home we can sort your rocks," said Uncle Jim.
"One day I'd like a collection like yours," said Hugh.

GO ROCK COLLECTING. Take a bag for collecting,
a magnifying glass, and a field guide to rocks.
Walk slowly and look carefully at the ground.
When you get home, sort your
rocks into different groups.

	Rock 1	Rock 2
Where found	Seaside	Backyard
Shape	Round	Flat
Color	White	Gray
Texture	Smooth	Rough
Hard or soft	Soft	Hard

QUIZ

What kind of materials are rocks, natural or manmade (made by humans)?
Answer on page 4

Which is the only **rock** that floats? Why is it so light?
Answers on page 9

What is **soil** made up of? What small animals live in the **soil**?
Answers on page 18

Which of these rocks do you think is a fossil, soft rock, tough rock, or a mineral?

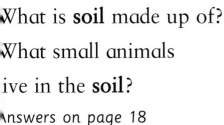

Answers on page 8, 11, 18, 22

INDEX